Wreck Trek

Angie Belcher
photographs by Andy Belcher

Learning Media

Contents

Introduction

Underwater wrecks have a special magic. When a ship or plane goes down at sea, it becomes a sort of time capsule, carrying a slice of history: weapons, tools, everyday objects, and cargo – perhaps even treasure. Sometimes, a wreck is the grave of the people who went down with it.

When they are discovered, many years or even centuries later, wrecks can provide fascinating clues about the way people lived and worked in the past.

1. Finding a Wreck

Most wrecks are lost forever under miles of dangerous ocean. Often no one knows exactly where the ship or plane went down. Even if they do, the wreck is hardly ever found on the seabed directly below that spot. Tides and currents move it, and mud and sand eventually bury it.

Sometimes, finding a wreck is just good luck. People fishing might snag their nets on it, or a diver might spot something unusual. Other times, it may take many hours of research and lots of money, equipment, and time to unlock the secrets buried by the sea long ago.

Once a wreck is found, its location must be carefully marked so that it is not lost again. A buoy is attached to a shallow wreck, or a GPS location is recorded for one lying in deep water.

Divers collect small items that might help to identify the wreck. **Marine archaeologists** mark out the site with grids and photograph each section. Computers record the position of everything that is taken from the site.

GPS (Global Positioning System)

A GPS uses signals bounced off space satellites to pinpoint where an item is. It can tell you exactly where something is, anywhere on the planet.

The *Mary Rose* was a warship built for King Henry VIII of England. In 1545, it sank during a battle. For over 400 years, it lay in the mud at the bottom of The Solent (near the English Channel). A few people tried to find it, but no one succeeded.

Then, in 1967, there was worldwide excitement when the *Mary Rose* was located. Much of the wooden structure had rotted away, but nearly half of the ancient ship – the part buried beneath the mud – was still in good condition.

Divers searching in the cabins discovered thousands of everyday objects – leather shoes and waistcoats, carpenters' tools, combs, cups, and bottles – as well as the remains of 200 men.

One of the most important finds was a medicine chest in the doctor's cabin. It contained jars of ointment, drug flasks, syringes, and many other things that showed what medical care for sailors was like in those days.

How a wreck breaks down

| 0 years | 50 years | 100 years | 200 years |

Wreck facts
- Cold water helps preserve wrecks.
- Wrecks in salt water break down faster than those in fresh water.
- Wrecks break down faster in shallow water because of the action of waves and sand.

2. Wreck Hunters

There are underwater wrecks all around the world – not only ancient sailing ships, but all kinds of boats and planes that have been lost at sea.

And there are people who spend most of their lives searching for wrecks. Some do it for a living, others do it for fun. They are driven by the hope of finding treasure, the adventure of diving, and their interest in special wrecks.

Mel Fisher set out in 1969 to find the *Nuestra Señora de Atocha*, a Spanish **galleon** that sank in the Straits of Florida in 1622. Explorers had tried many times over the years to find the wreck and its treasure, without success.

With the help of historical records and old maps, Mel worked out where to search with his magnetometer. His first find was a huge anchor with a solid gold chain wrapped around it. Nearby were gold bars, guns, a Spanish **musket** ball, and many coins – but no ship.

It wasn't until 1985, sixteen years after he began searching, that Mel Fisher found the scattered remains of the *Atocha*.

Magnetometer
A magnetometer is like a giant magnet, which is towed behind a boat and detects metal on the seabed. It is useful for finding scraps of shipwrecks, such as anchors, **hulls**, and cannons.

Its cargo was the richest treasure find since **King Tutankhamen**'s tomb. For Mel, it was "finders keepers" since the *Atocha* had been abandoned long ago by the Spanish and it lay outside United States waters.

The fabulous treasures from the *Atocha* are displayed in the Mel Fisher Maritime Museum in Florida. Some have been collected into an exhibition that travels around the world.

Robert Ballard wasn't after treasure. Ever since he was a boy, he had dreamed of finding the *Titanic*, the most famous wreck in history. The luxury liner sank after hitting an iceberg on its very first voyage, on 15 April 1912. More than 1,500 people died.

Ballard worked out where the wreck of the *Titanic* might be. In 1985 he led an expedition to the area. For weeks he searched with *Argo*, a small ROV (remote-operated vehicle).

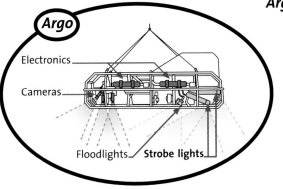

Argo

Electronics

Cameras

Floodlights / **Strobe lights**

Argo finds the Titanic

surface

1 mile

2 miles

12,460 feet

Titanic

Argo

Argo uses video cameras to find hidden objects in deep water. With only four days of the expedition left, some exciting images were sent to the surface. They showed the *Titanic* lying 2¹/₂ miles below the surface of the Atlantic Ocean.

A year later he was back. This time he wanted to visit the wreck himself. Ballard and his two crew squeezed into a mini-submarine called *Alvin*. An ROV named *Jason Junior*, armed with cameras and video recorders, was attached to *Alvin*.

The depth of the *Titanic* compared with the height of the Eiffel Tower (Paris, France) and the Sears Tower (Chicago, U.S.A).

11

It took *Alvin* 2¹/₂ hours to sink to the ocean floor. Ballard and his crew spent four hours exploring the wreck. They found that the *Titanic* had broken in two. They didn't find the huge hole that people expected to be there, but they did find buckled and torn steel plates from the side of the ship. Perhaps the force of the collision with the iceberg had burst the steel plates apart, letting the water rush in.

While *Alvin* rested on the *Titanic*'s deck, the crew guided *Jason Junior* inside the wreck. It took photographs of the grand staircase, the **chandeliers**, and the ship's safe.

Ballard believed that nothing should be

removed from the wreck. As the team left the *Titanic* for the last time, *Alvin* released a plaque in memory of the people who had died. Slowly, silently, it sank to rest on the deck.

The *Titanic* sinks

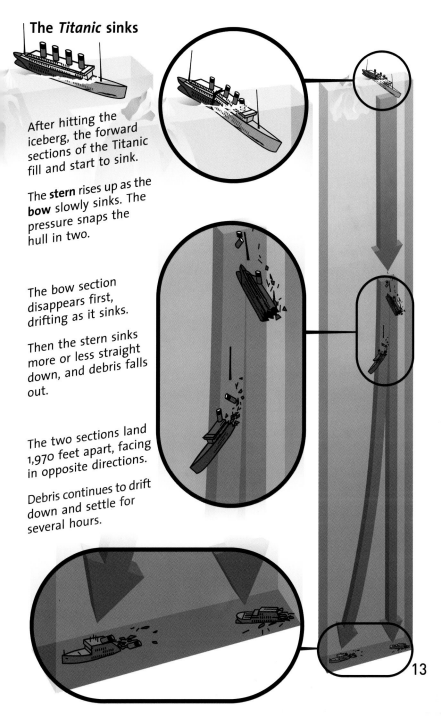

After hitting the iceberg, the forward sections of the Titanic fill and start to sink.

The **stern** rises up as the **bow** slowly sinks. The pressure snaps the hull in two.

The bow section disappears first, drifting as it sinks.

Then the stern sinks more or less straight down, and debris falls out.

The two sections land 1,970 feet apart, facing in opposite directions.

Debris continues to drift down and settle for several hours.

13

Not everyone agreed that the wreck should be left in peace. After a French group retrieved some items from the wreck, a law was passed in the United States making the *Titanic* an international memorial. It became illegal to sell *Titanic* **artifacts** within the United States.

Who owns a wreck?
If a wreck hunter can prove that the owners of a wreck have abandoned it, then it belongs to them. Otherwise, they can claim a reward. Many of the artifacts taken from wrecks are displayed in museums. They are a memorial to the people who drowned.

ROVs (Remote-Operated Vehicles)

ROVs such as *Jason Junior* and *Argo* are used for deep, dangerous work and can do almost anything a diver can do, without the risks. There are no crew on an ROV. It is controlled by a cable linked to a "mother ship" on the surface. Pictures from the ROV's video cameras are sent to the ship so that the pilot can see what is going on.

Argo is like a steel sled the size of a small car. *Jason Junior* is about half that size.

Submersibles

A one-person submersible is like a cross between a diving suit and a submarine. The diver is lowered into the water on strong cables. Inside the suit, the diver uses foot switches to control the submersible's movements. The diver can talk to the people on the ship above, and breathe air at normal pressure.

Mini-submarines carry more than one person. *Alvin* is 25 feet long and 9 feet wide. It has remote-controlled arms, cameras and lights, computers for collecting information, and instruments for measuring water temperatures, currents, and depths.

If a wreck is unusually important, professional searchers may call in the United States Navy's nuclear submarine *NR-1*. It can dive to 2,600 feet and look around using **sonar**. *NR-1* was used to help find the wreck of the *Britannic* (sister ship to the *Titanic*) and the wreckage of the space shuttle *Challenger*.

3. Silent Warriors

Not all wrecks are sunk by storm or accident. The two world wars left the ocean floor littered with hundreds of troop ships, planes, and submarines. When these wrecks lie in shallow water they are popular sites for recreational **scuba divers**.

Black Jack

The B17 Flying Fortress was one of the largest planes used during World War II. One of these planes got the nickname *Black Jack* from its last two serial numbers, 21 — the lucky number in the card game Blackjack. But *Black Jack*'s luck ran out on a mission to Papua New Guinea. After dropping its bombs, dodging enemy fighters, and flying through a violent storm, Black Jack developed engine trouble. Then it ran out of fuel and crashed into the ocean at 125 miles per hour. The crew were rescued by nearby islanders.

Divers discovered the wreck of *Black Jack*, still in one piece, in 1986. They identified it by checking old war records.

The *President Coolidge*

During World War II, many large passenger ships were converted into troop ships. The *President Coolidge* had all its fancy extras removed and was refitted with enough bunks, weapons, and supplies to transport 5,000 soldiers to war in the Pacific.

As the boat entered Santo Harbor in Vanuatu, it hit two mines. The captain steered the boat onto a reef close to shore. The troops scrambled down nets and onto life rafts, just in time. The ship slid back off the reef and sank.

Today, the *President Coolidge* is the largest wreck dive site in the world and the easiest for divers to get to. It is like an underwater war museum. Rifles, bayonets, helmets, and gas masks still lie on the decks where they fell. Going deeper, divers can see the jeeps and trucks stacked in its holds.

4. From Wreck to Reef

When a ship or plane sinks, it creates a new home for all kinds of sea creatures. Within hours, small plants and animals attach themselves to the wreck. These attract larger animals. Eventually, there is a whole underwater community living in every nook and cranny of the wreck.

Some of these artificial reefs are protected as marine reserves. This means that visitors may look at the marine life, but they are not allowed to touch any of it. Marine reserves provide a safe place for plants and animals to grow and reproduce, and are useful for scientific study.

The *Rainbow Warrior*

A famous wreck that has become a reef is the *Rainbow Warrior*. The ship belonged to the environmental action group Greenpeace. In 1985, while the *Rainbow Warrior* was in New Zealand preparing to sail to Mururoa Atoll to protest against French nuclear tests, it was blown up by French secret agents. The Greenpeace photographer was killed as he tried to save his cameras.

The wreck was refloated and two years later was towed to a safe, sheltered area and sunk to make an artificial reef. Now the *Rainbow Warrior* attracts divers from all around the world. It is completely covered in colorful algae and anemones – a living rainbow.

The *Tui*

The *Tui* used to belong to the United States Navy. Old and out of date, it waited to be broken down as scrap metal. But a group of divers had another idea. They wanted it **scuttled** to create a reef. They convinced the authorities that this was a good idea and bought the *Tui* for one American silver dollar.

First the Navy removed the *Tui*'s two big engines. Its fuel tanks were cleaned out, and all loose items were removed. Welders sealed shut every area of the ship that could be dangerous for divers and cut large holes just above the boat's **waterline**.

Finally a tugboat towed it out into the chosen position. Seawater was pumped into its holds. The ship sat lower and lower, until the waterline reached the gaping holes in the hull. Water poured in, and the *Tui* sank gracefully to the sea floor.

Divers can enter the wreck from many areas. One of the most popular ways is to swim down the smokestack into the engine room or come out part way down through a hole.

Divers who have special training in wreck diving can take flashlights, lines, and reels and investigate the inside corridors. They need to be careful – it is easy to become lost and confused when diving in large wrecks. They must constantly check their depth, time, and air supply to be sure of a safe return.

The *Mikhail Lermontov*

When the Russian cruise ship *Mikhail Lermontov* took a short cut through a narrow passage in the Marlborough Sounds in New Zealand in 1986, shallow rocks gouged a hole in its side. It was a frightening experience for the passengers, who were rescued by local boats as the luxury liner sank. One person died.

Unfortunately, four more lives have been lost on the *Mikhail Lermontov* since then, by wreck divers who did not take enough care. In a ship of this size it is easy to become lost.

Swimming around the outside, divers can see anchors, giant propellers, radar and navigation gear, and the huge smokestack.

Inside, it is dark, deep, and scary. Because the ship is lying on its side, the ballroom looks like an undersea cliff with tables poking out of it. The swimming pool is still inside a glass enclosure and has signs that read "No Diving Please" and "Caution! The Pool is Empty."

Diving data

- The pressure on a diver at a depth of 33 feet is twice as much as the pressure at the surface.
- A mask helps a diver to see clearly underwater by creating an airspace between their eyes and the water.
- Things underwater look 25% larger.
- Sound travels four times faster underwater.
- Our bodies lose heat 25% faster in water than on land.

Dangers of wreck diving

You don't have to be a trained wreck diver to visit many of the wrecks in shallow water, but you do need to take great care.

- Divers must be careful to avoid sharp edges and rough surfaces that might cut them or damage their equipment.
- Over the years, a wreck can become covered in a tangle of old nets and fishing lines. Divers have to be careful not to get caught on these.
- When wrecks are in deep waters and areas with strong currents, divers must take extra care to check their air supply.
- Divers who enter wrecks without wreck training and experience, or proper equipment, are in danger of getting lost in the underwater maze. It is always risky for a diver to lose sight of the place where they entered a wreck.

5. Up from the Depths

Most sunken wrecks never rise above the ocean surface again. It is too difficult and dangerous to bring them up, and they usually can't be repaired. But some wrecks have to be **salvaged** because it is too dangerous to leave them where they are. Wrecks that are leaking oil, carrying hazardous cargos, or blocking shipping lanes all have to be removed. This is a job for experts. Divers with special training take the wreck and its cargo apart bit by bit, then take the pieces away.

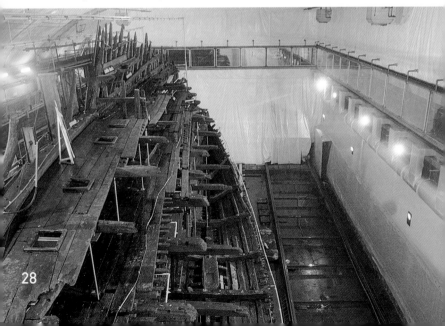

Salvaging the *Mary Rose*

Occasionally, a shipwreck is salvaged because it is of special interest – like the *Mary Rose*. This was such an important find that it was decided to bring the whole ship back to the surface so that many more people would be able to see it.

(1) After all the artifacts and loose pieces were brought to the surface, the hull was raised a few inches each day using a lifting frame (shown in orange) and hydraulic jacks (green).

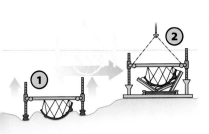

(2) When it was clear of the seabed, the wreck was shifted onto a lifting cradle (yellow) using a floating crane.

(3) Then the hull was raised to the surface, wrapped in foam and plastic, and sprayed with special chemicals to prevent it crumbling in the air.

(4) Finally, it was taken to the Portsmouth Naval Base where a special museum was built to display the hull (see photo on page 28) and many of the 20,000 artifacts that were found on the wreck (see pages 6 and 7).

Wreck locations

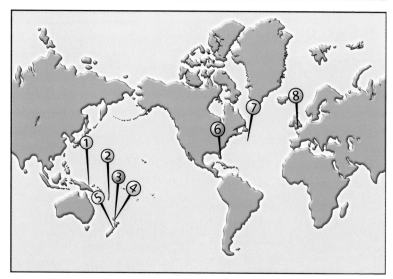

① *Black Jack* – Papua New Guinea

② *President Coolidge* – Vanuatu

③ *Rainbow Warrior* – New Zealand

④ *Tui* – New Zealand

⑤ *Mikhail Lermontov* – New Zealand

⑥ *Atocha* – U.S.A.

⑦ *Titanic* – Atlantic Ocean

⑧ *Mary Rose* – England

Websites

You can use the Internet to find out more about wrecks and wreck exploration. Try these websites:

http://www.jasonproject.org
http://www.maryrose.org
http://www.melfisher.com
http://www.titanic-online.com

Glossary

(These words are printed in bold type the first time they appear in the book.)

artifacts ▷ objects made by people

bow ▷ the front end of a boat or ship

chandelier ▷ a decorative light fitting made of glass

galleon ▷ a sailing ship of the 15th–17th centuries

hull ▷ the frame or body of a ship

King Tutankhamen ▷ an Egyptian pharaoh whose tomb contained fabulous treasures

marine archaeologist ▷ a scientist who studies ancient cultural objects found in the sea

musket ▷ an old-fashioned rifle

salvage ▷ to recover a vessel or its contents from the sea

scuba divers ▷ divers using self-contained underwater breathing apparatus

scuttle ▷ to sink deliberately

sonar ▷ a machine that uses sound waves to find things

stern ▷ the rear end of a boat or ship

strobe lights ▷ lights that go on and off very quickly

waterline ▷ the imaginary line around a ship's hull made by the surface of the water

Index